The Ancient City of Rome

Ancient History Grade 6
Children's Ancient History

BABY PROFESSOR

EDUCATION KIDS

Speedy Publishing LLC

40 E. Main St. #1156

Newark, DE 19711

www.speedypublishing.com

Copyright 2017

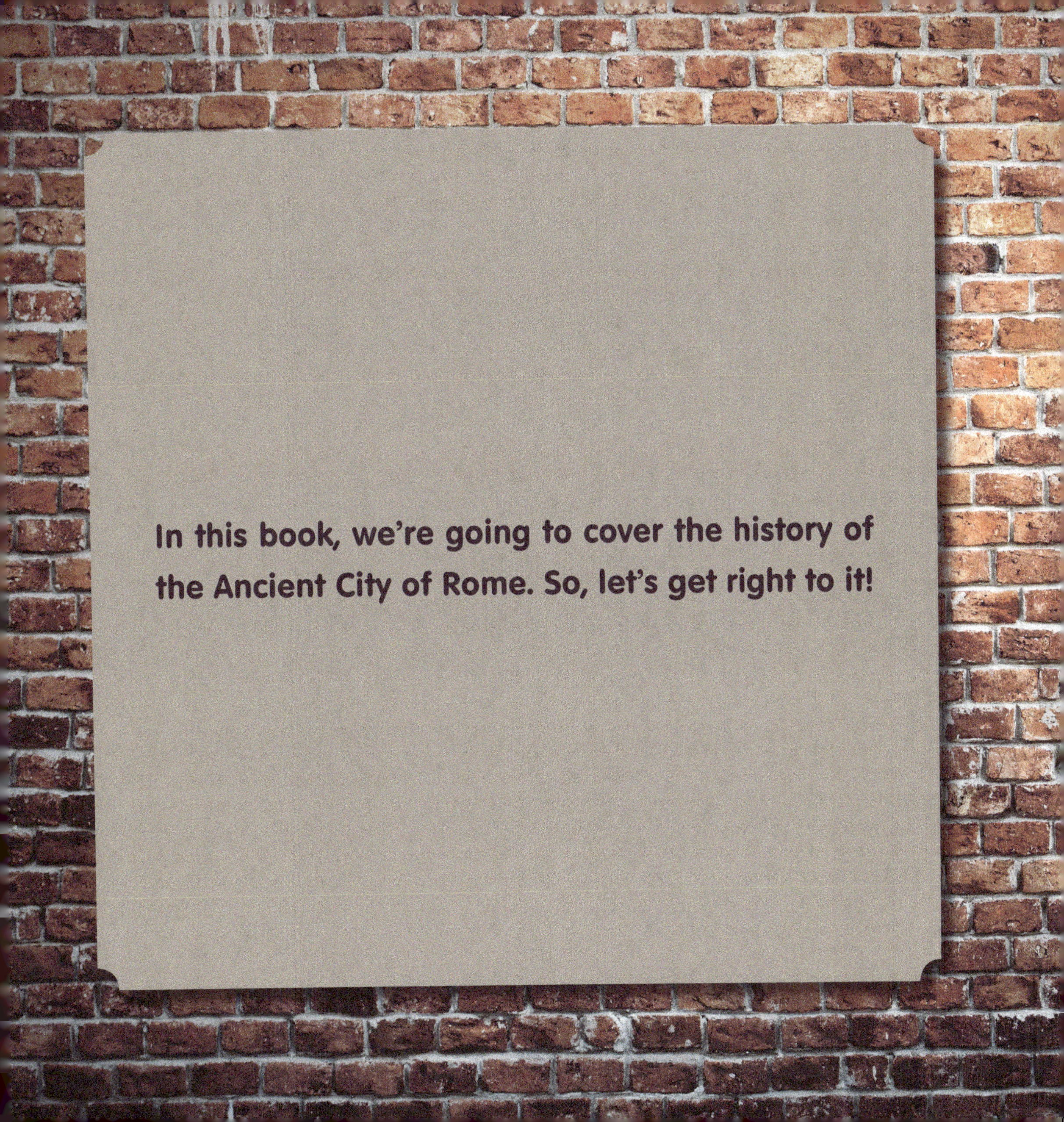

In this book, we're going to cover the history of
the Ancient City of Rome. So, let's get right to it!

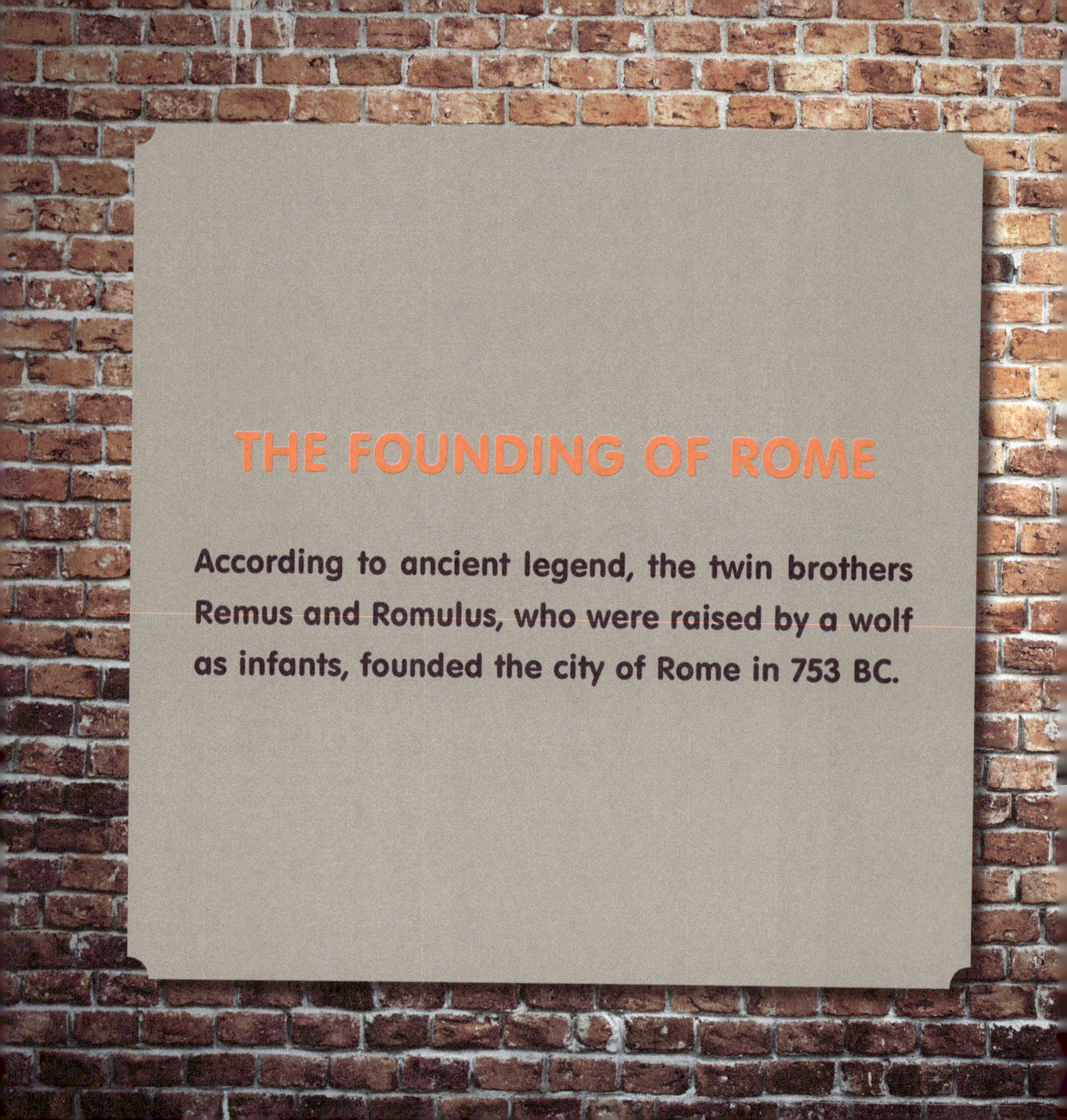

THE FOUNDING OF ROME

According to ancient legend, the twin brothers
Remus and Romulus, who were raised by a wolf
as infants, founded the city of Rome in 753 BC.

Mount Aventine

They couldn't decide whether the city should be built on Aventine Hill or Palatine Hill. To settle the issue, they decided to use augury, a process of observing the flight of birds to determine a good omen. Remus sat on Aventine Hill and waited and Romulus sat on Palatine Hill and waited.

Then, Remus saw six birds. He knew the city should be built at Aventine Hill, but, in the meantime, Romulus had seen twelve birds. Romulus thought they should build at Palatine because he had seen six more birds, but Remus objected because he had seen his birds first. They still couldn't decide. Romulus got tired of waiting and started to dig trenches and build walls at Palatine Hill.

Lungotevere Aventino

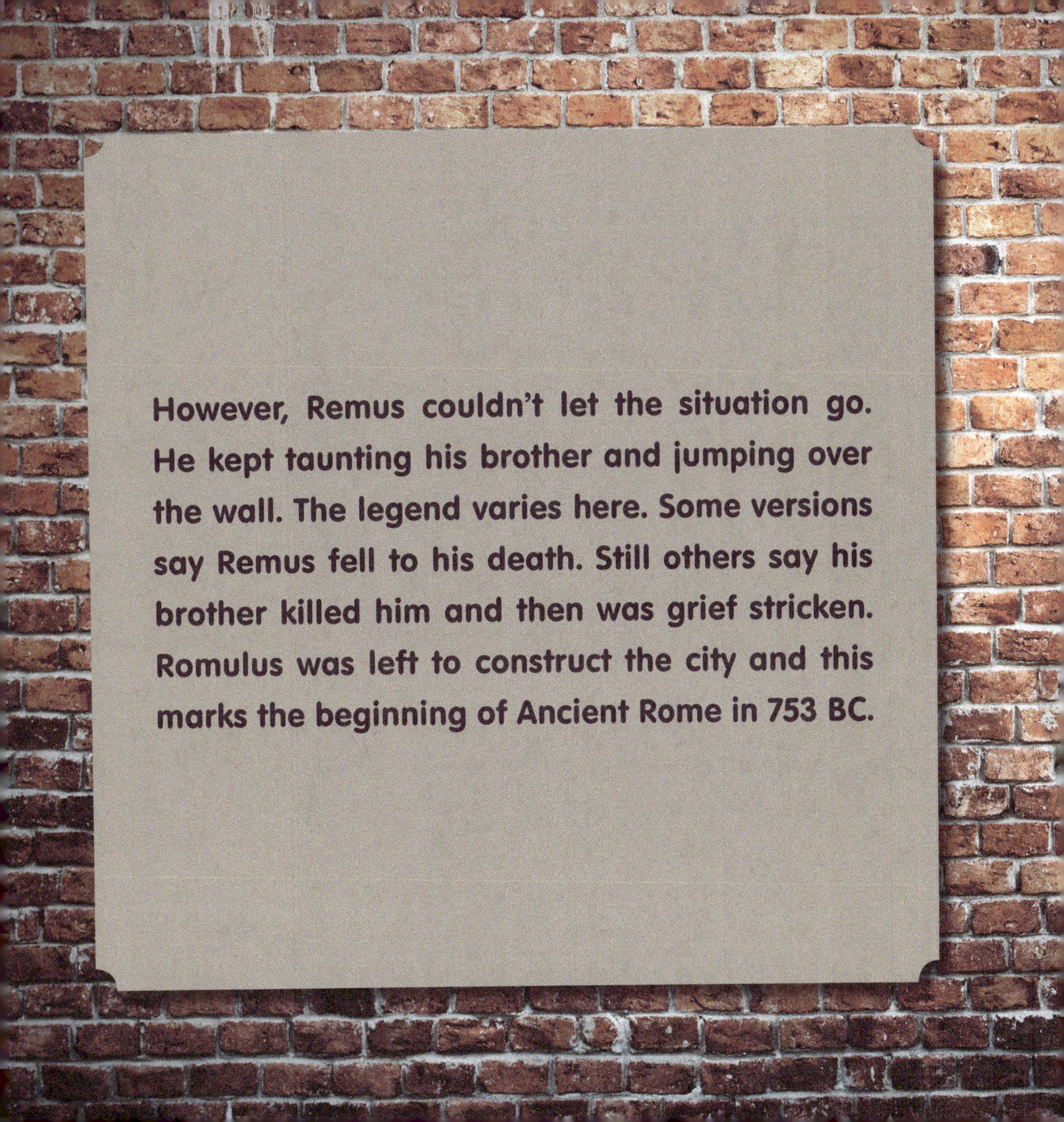
However, Remus couldn't let the situation go.
He kept taunting his brother and jumping over
the wall. The legend varies here. Some versions
say Remus fell to his death. Still others say his
brother killed him and then was grief stricken.
Romulus was left to construct the city and this
marks the beginning of Ancient Rome in 753 BC.

This is not the only legend about the founding of Rome, although it's the best known. Another legend claims that the city was named after a woman called Roma, who had traveled with Aeneas, the famous Trojan hero from Greek mythology. They had traveled to the area after the fall of the city of Troy.

City of Troy

River Tiber

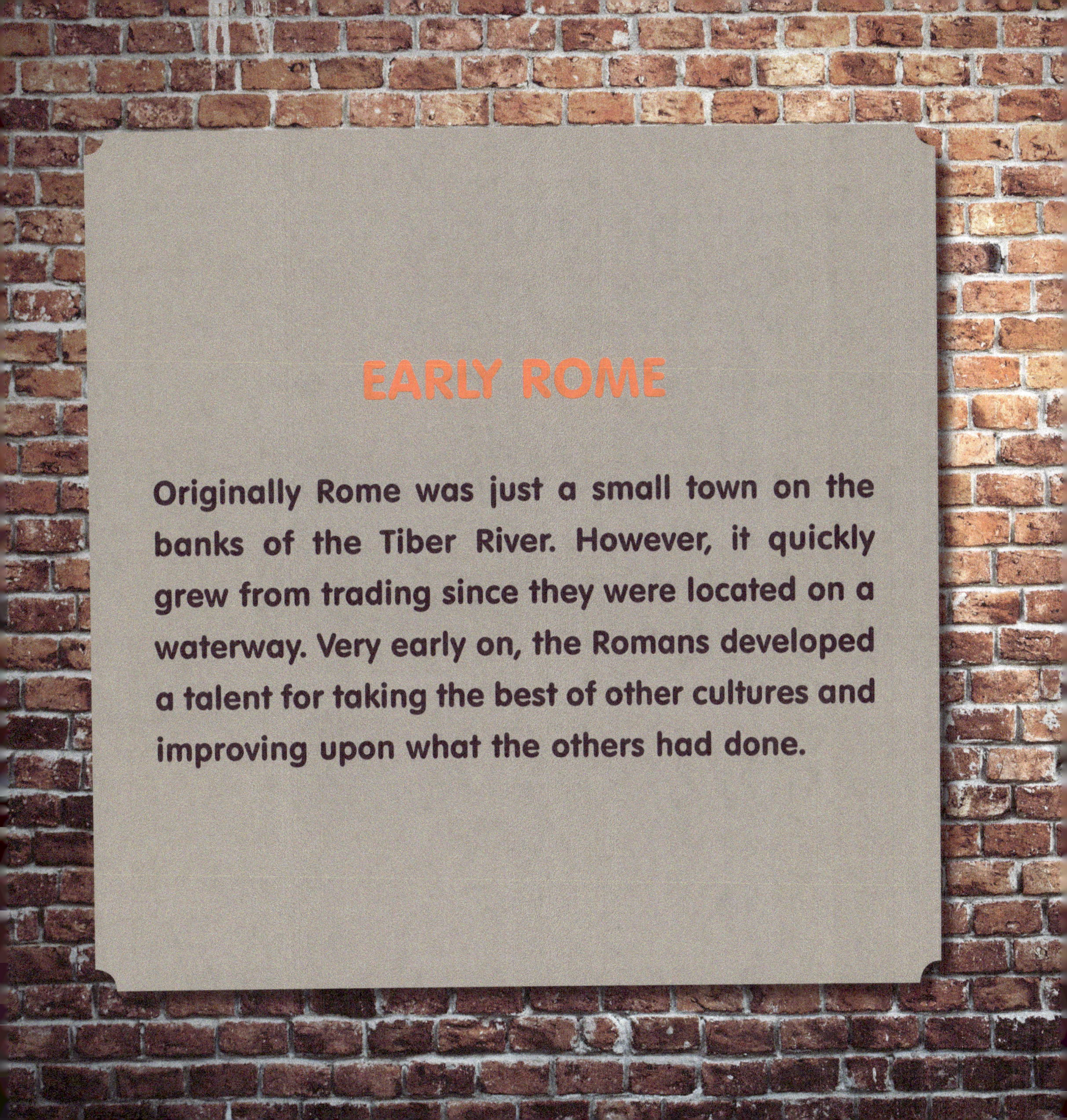

EARLY ROME

Originally Rome was just a small town on the banks of the Tiber River. However, it quickly grew from trading since they were located on a waterway. Very early on, the Romans developed a talent for taking the best of other cultures and improving upon what the others had done.

At that time, south of Rome, Greek civilization was at its height, and the early Romans greatly admired the Greeks. They absorbed and adapted Greek culture, literature, and religion to suit their own. They also took the best of Greek architecture with its towering columns and ornate sculptures. The Etruscan culture was to the north of Rome and from the Etruscans, the Romans learned the buying and selling of imports and exports.

Roman Forum

It's not clear whether the Etruscans taught these skills to the Romans or the Romans just learned them from watching the Etruscans. Around 600 AD, the town of Rome had grown into a very prosperous trading city. When Tarquin the Proud, the last of Rome's seven kings, was deposed, Lucius Junius Brutus took over the government and reformed the system from a monarchy to a republic in 509 BC.

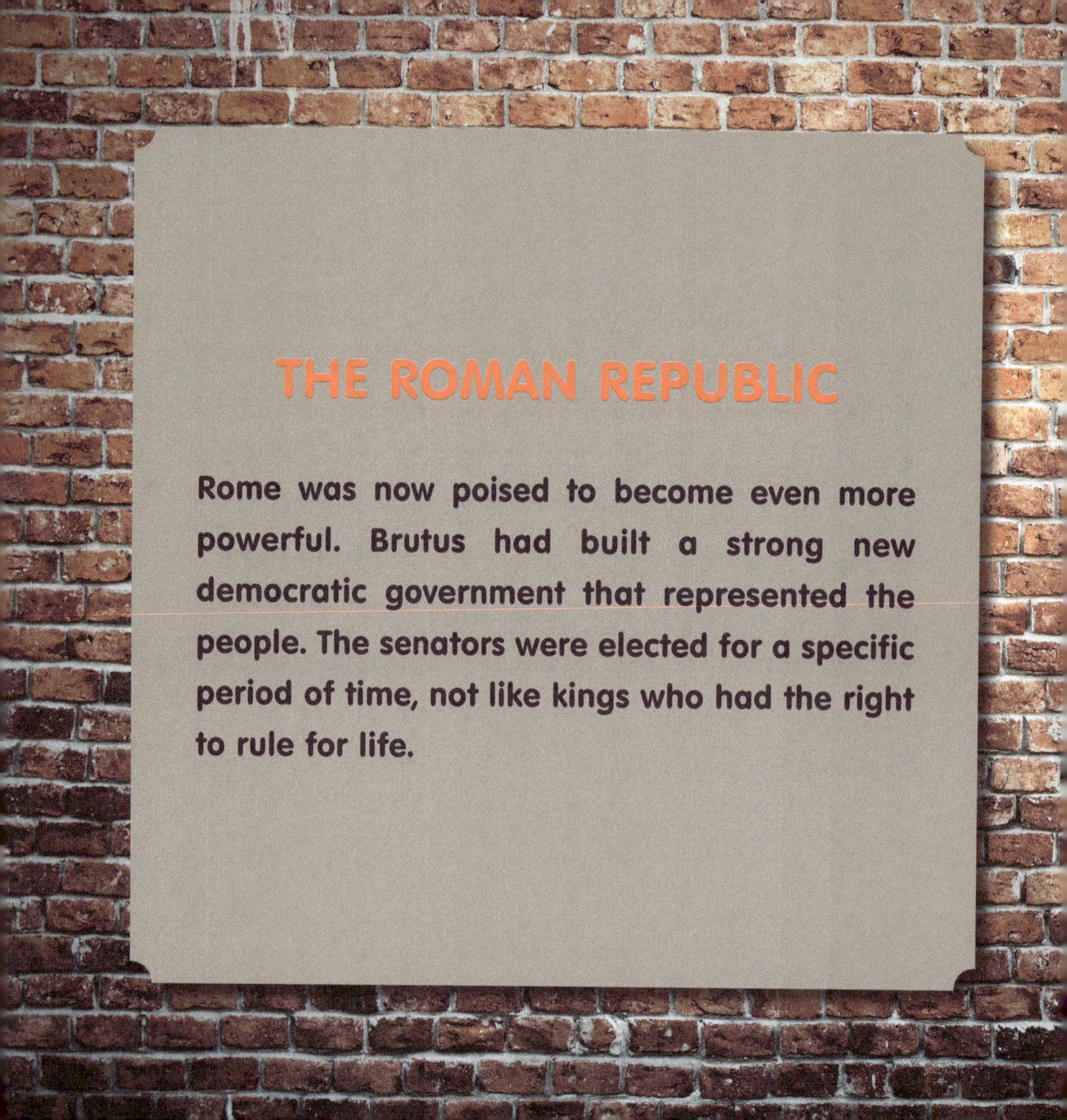

THE ROMAN REPUBLIC

Rome was now poised to become even more powerful. Brutus had built a strong new democratic government that represented the people. The senators were elected for a specific period of time, not like kings who had the right to rule for life.

Imperial Forums

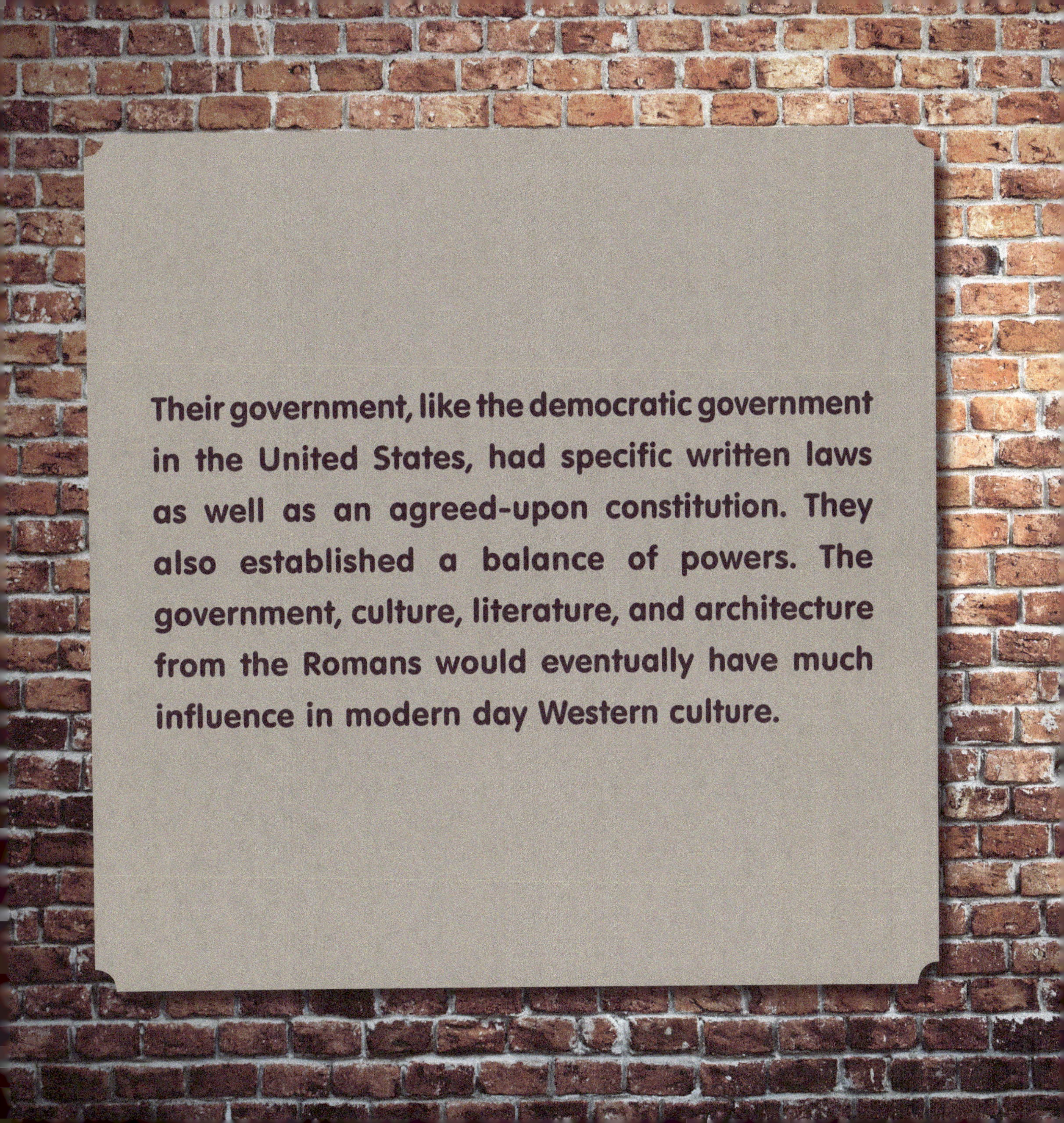

Their government, like the democratic government in the United States, had specific written laws as well as an agreed-upon constitution. They also established a balance of powers. The government, culture, literature, and architecture from the Romans would eventually have much influence in modern day Western culture.

The Republic was the official government of Rome from its creation in 509 BC to 45 BC. With their new innovative government in place, the Romans were now ready to start their quest to conquer.

Basilica Maxentius

WAR AND EXPANSION

The first major wars that consolidated the city's power were the Punic Wars beginning in 264 BC and ending in 146 BC. Rome won against its enemy and rival, the North African city of Carthage. Other than the occasional interference by pirates, Rome now had domain over the Western Mediterranean. The war conquests meant that Rome had so many slaves that the regular citizens were sometimes unemployed, leading to unrest and crime. Relationships between the two major social classes in Rome were becoming more strained.

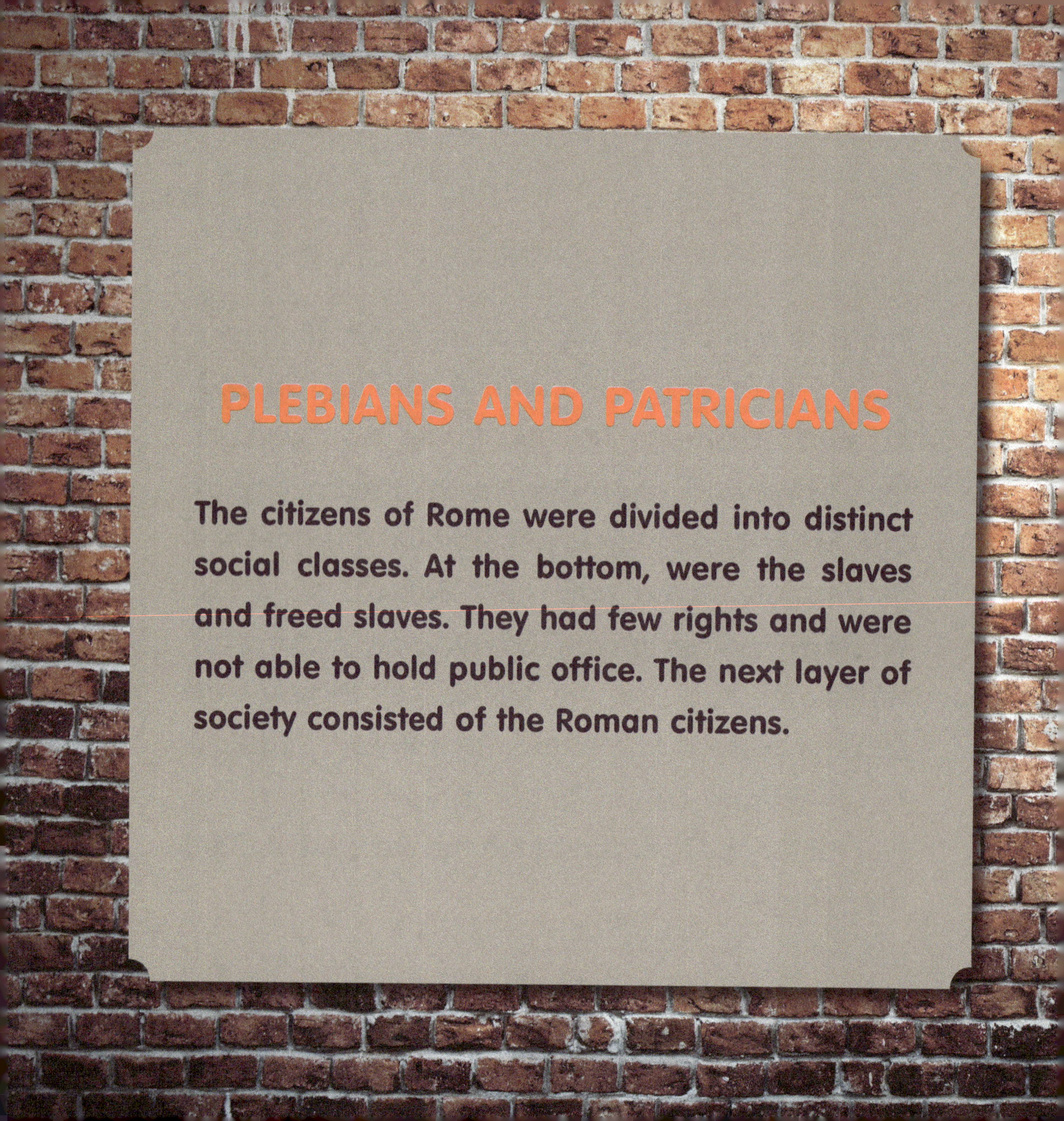

PLEBIANS AND PATRICIANS

The citizens of Rome were divided into distinct social classes. At the bottom, were the slaves and freed slaves. They had few rights and were not able to hold public office. The next layer of society consisted of the Roman citizens.

They fell into two distinct categories: the plebians and the patricians. Today, the word "plebian" means commonplace or ordinary. The plebians were the soldiers, skilled laborers, farmers, and craftsmen of the city. The patricians were the elite and wealthy citizens. In Ancient Rome, you had to be a descendent of a patrician to become a patrician. Their ancestors were the senators who had represented the people in the first Senate. Even though the patricians were such a small segment of the population, they had the land, the political power, and the wealth. During these early times, plebians or plebs were not allowed to marry patricians or to hold public office.

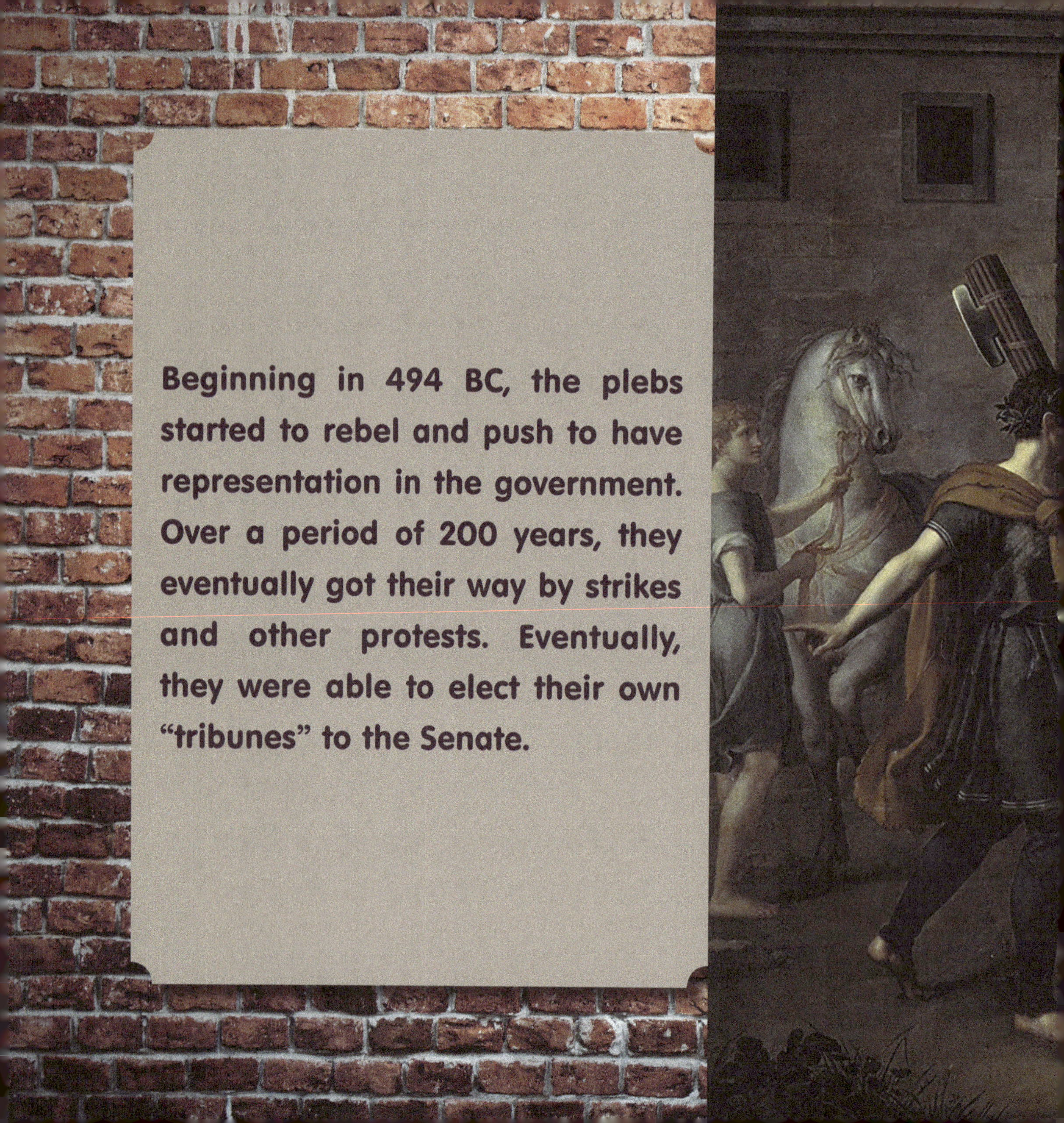

Beginning in 494 BC, the plebs started to rebel and push to have representation in the government. Over a period of 200 years, they eventually got their way by strikes and other protests. Eventually, they were able to elect their own "tribunes" to the Senate.

At the end of this time period, two brothers who were Roman tribunes lead an uprising for reforms. They lost their lives but their cause resulted in land and political reforms and for a time curbed the Senate from corruption.

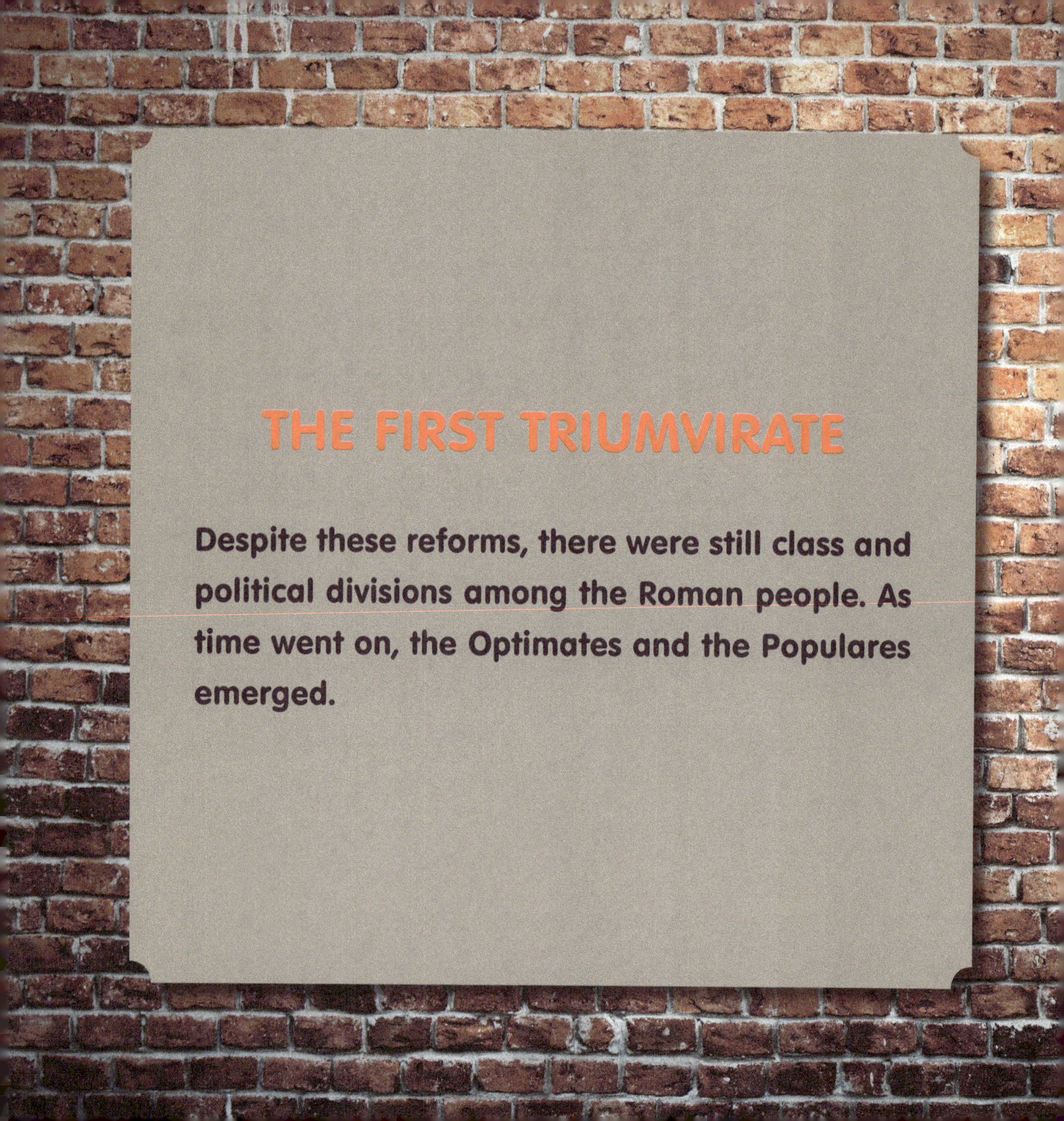

THE FIRST TRIUMVIRATE

Despite these reforms, there were still class and political divisions among the Roman people. As time went on, the Optimates and the Populares emerged.

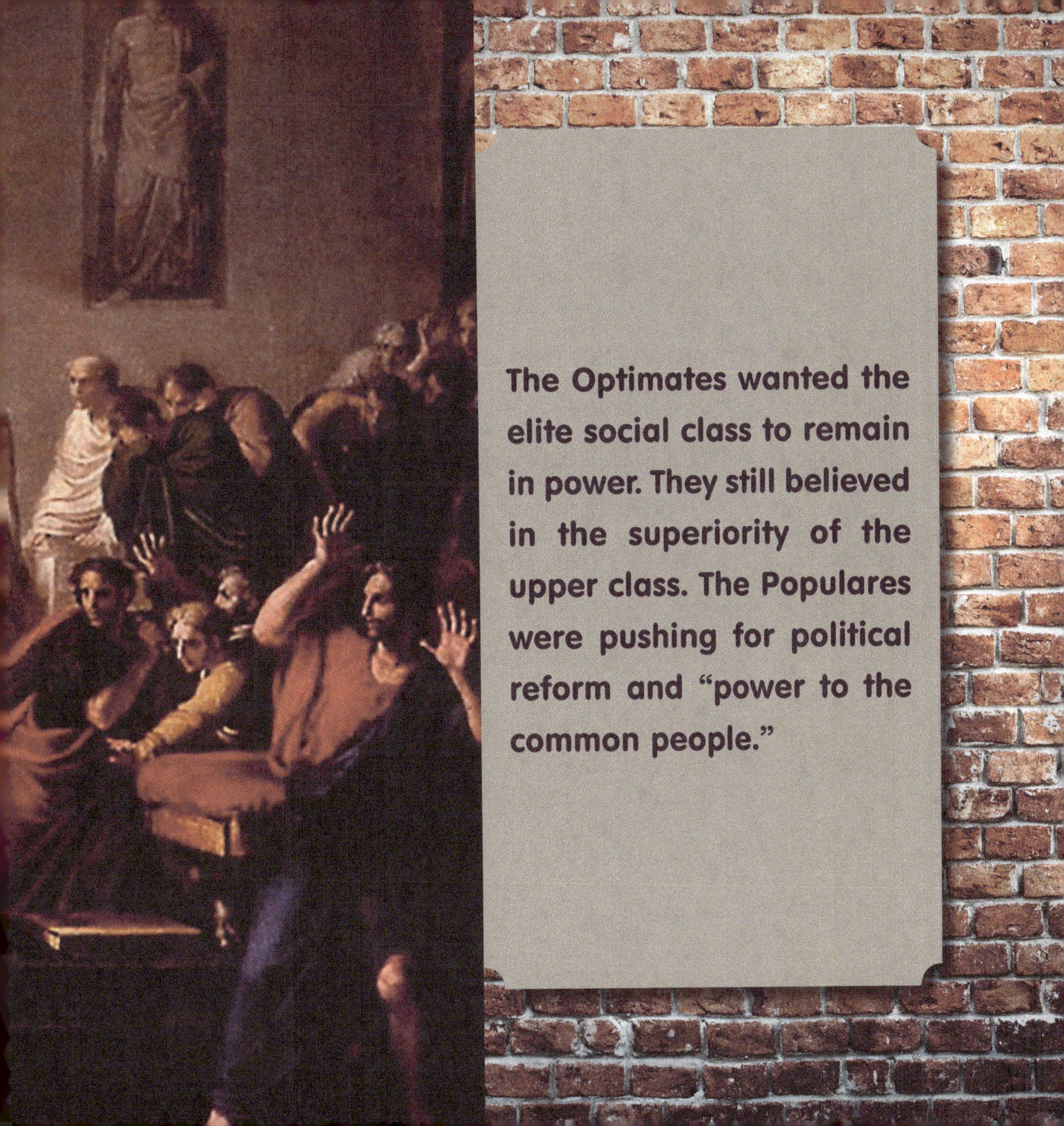

The Optimates wanted the elite social class to remain in power. They still believed in the superiority of the upper class. The Populares were pushing for political reform and "power to the common people."

This unrest would set the stage for three powerful men: Marcus Licinius Craccus, Gnaeus Pompeius Magnus, later known as Pompey the Great, and the young Julius Caesar. Though they weren't called this at the time, these three powerful men with different philosophies held all the power and today are called the first triumvirate. Crassus and Pompey were Optimates and Caesar was a Populare.

Both Pompey and Caesar were highly successful generals but when Craccus tried to earn the same level of prestige for himself, he was defeated and killed in battle.

Now it was just Pompey and Caesar and when Pompey tried to get rid of Caesar with a lawsuit, Caesar responded by crossing the Rubicon River and entering Rome at the head of his army. In 49 BC, the two met in battle in Greece and Caesar's smaller army defeated Pompey and his army. News of Caesar's victory quickly spread and many of Pompey's supporters switched sides to support Caesar.

M·AGRIPPA·L·F·COS·TERTIVM·FECIT

Caesar now held most of the power in Rome. Ironically, the "power to the people" that he had supported, he also brought to an end by proclaiming himself as a dictator. His leadership brought increased wealth to the city. He was tremendously popular among the people of Rome, but in 44 BC, he was killed by a group of conspirators, including Brutus and Cassius. This group feared that Caesar had too much power and might eventually abolish the Senate.

After Caesar's death, these three men took over and formed the Second Triumvirate, after they defeated Caesar's assassins.

Forum of Caesar

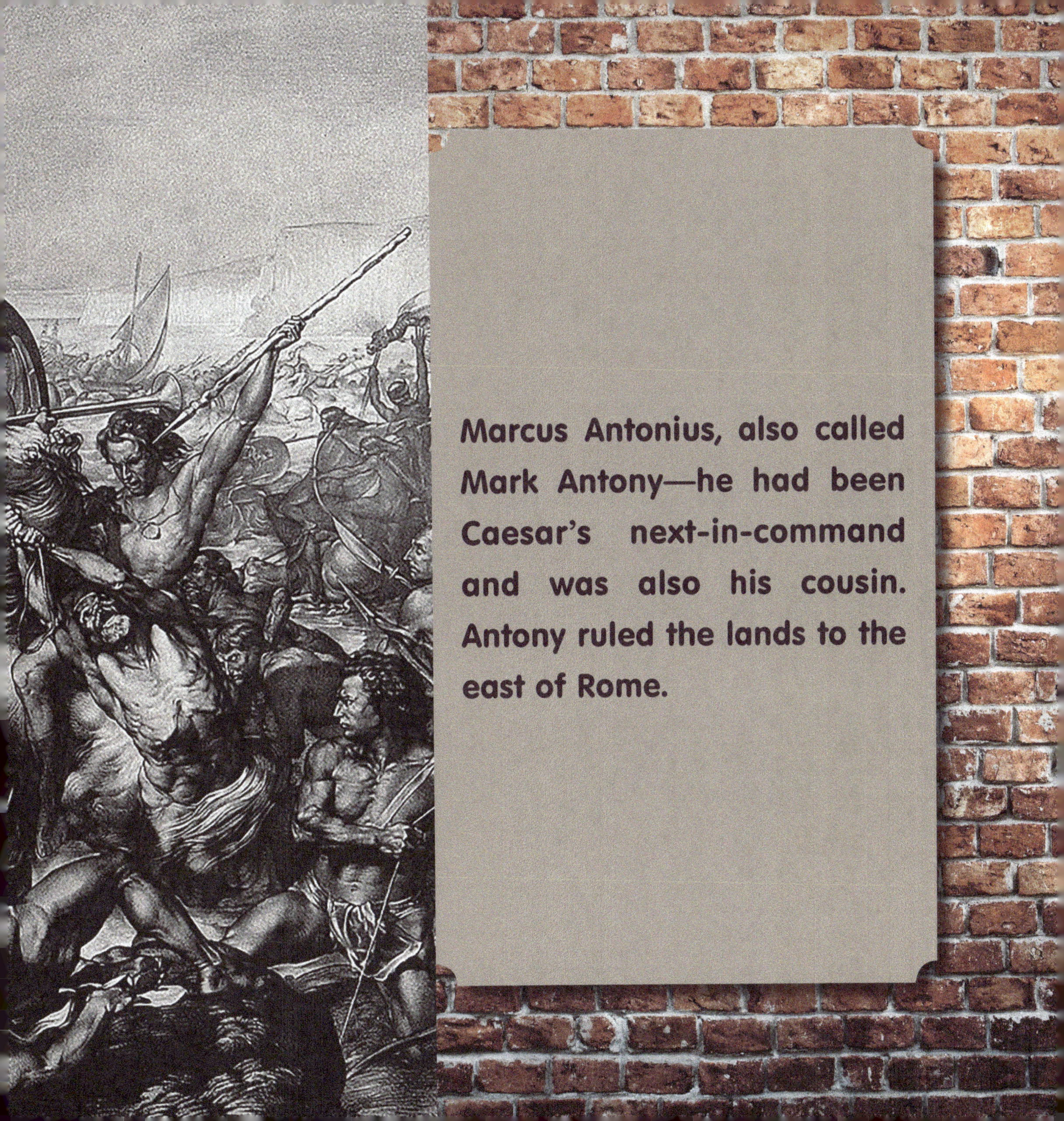

Marcus Antonius, also called Mark Antony—he had been Caesar's next-in-command and was also his cousin. Antony ruled the lands to the east of Rome.

Gaius Octavius Thurinus, also called Octavian—he was Caesar's nephew and also his heir. Octavian ruled the lands to the west.

Gaius Octavius

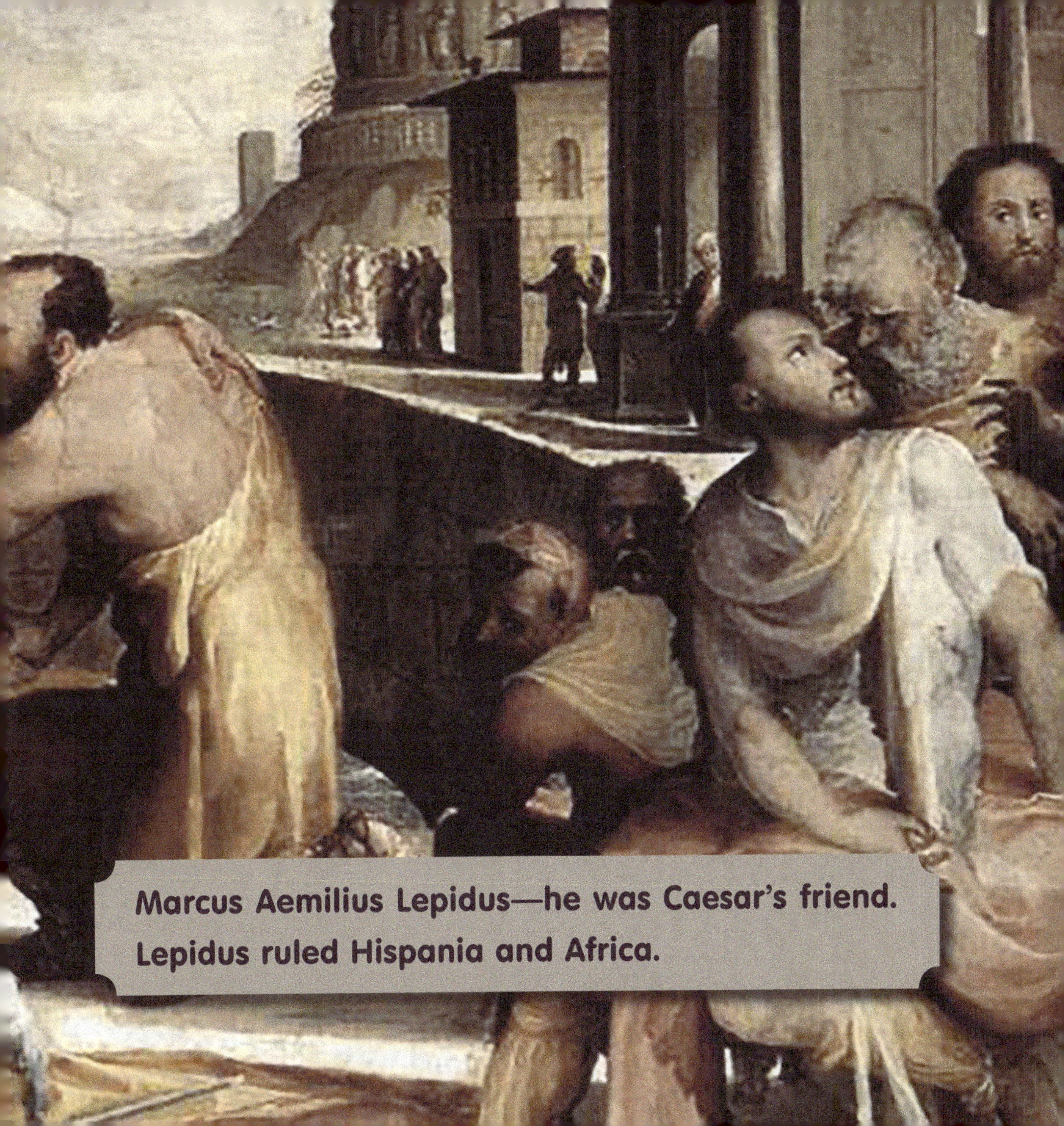

Marcus Aemilius Lepidus—he was Caesar's friend.
Lepidus ruled Hispania and Africa.

However, when Antony became involved with Egypt's powerful Queen, Cleopatra, the balance was upset and he and Octavian went to war. Even with the assistance of Egyptian forces, Antony lost and Antony and Cleopatra took their own lives. In 27 BC, Octavian was given new powers by the Senate and became the first Emperor of Rome. He changed his name to Augustus to represent his victory and newfound power. This event represents the end of Ancient Roman history and the beginning of the Roman Empire.

Cleopatra

The city of Rome is Italy's capital today. It is located on the same site as the ancient city. Ruins of many of the original buildings, such as the Colosseum, which was the event amphitheater, the Roman Forum, which was the central plaza surrounded by government buildings, and the Pantheon, which was formerly a temple, are still there.

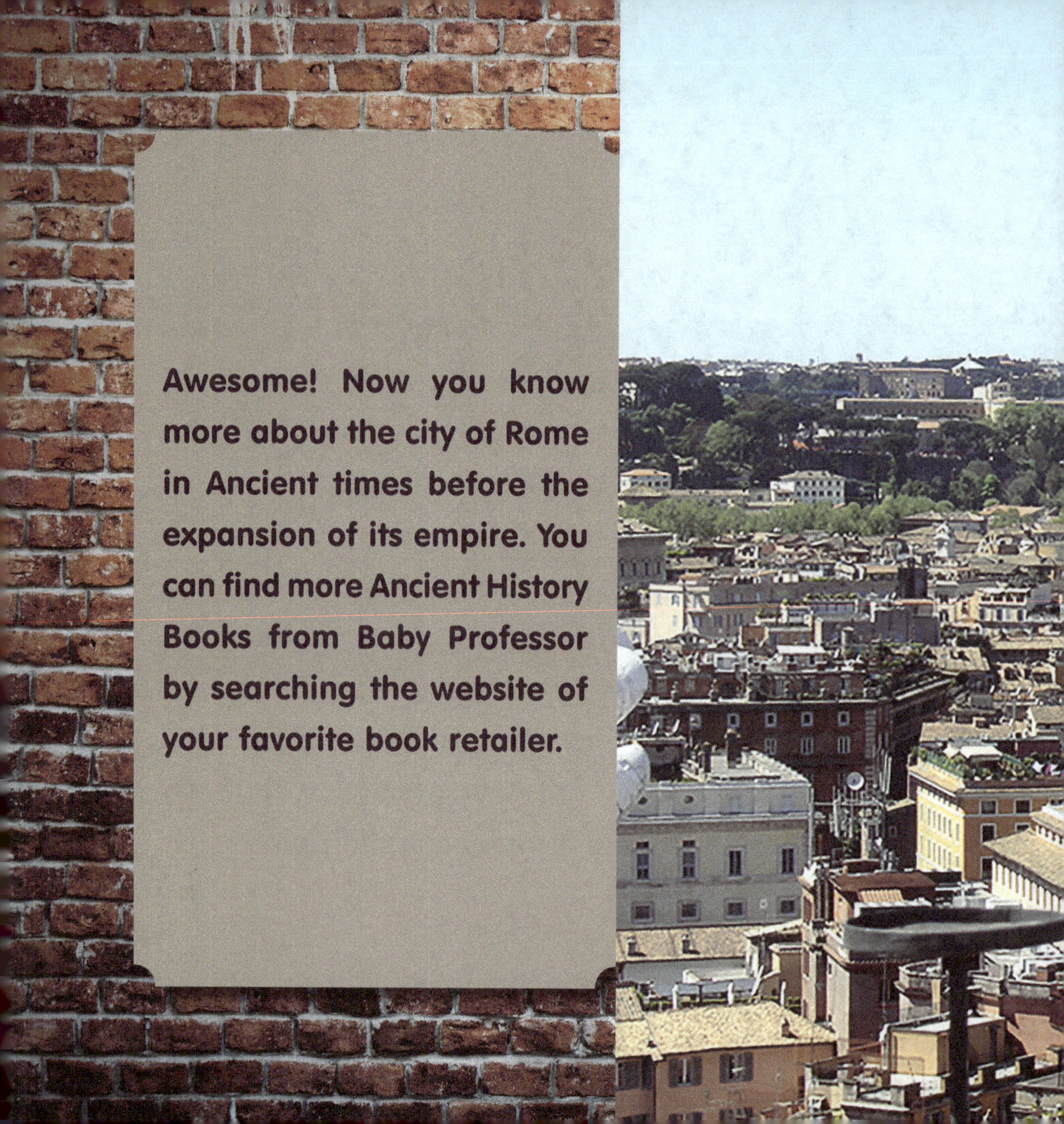

Awesome! Now you know more about the city of Rome in Ancient times before the expansion of its empire. You can find more Ancient History Books from Baby Professor by searching the website of your favorite book retailer.

Visit
BABY PROFESSOR
EDUCATION KIDS
www.BabyProfessorBooks.com
to download Free Baby Professor eBooks
and view our catalog of new and exciting
Children's Books

9 798869 432827